WALKING IN
VICTORY
A study on Joshua

Special thanks to:
Photos from: unsplash.com
Recipes from: Vladana Hořelková

Unless otherwise directed in writing by the Publisher, Scripture quotations are from the ESV® Bible (*The Holy Bible, English Standard Version®*), copyright 2001 by Crossway, a publishing ministry of Good News Publishers. Used by permission. All rights reserved.

Printed in the United States of America

Library of Congress Cataloging-in-Publication Data

Printed in the United States of America

24   23   22   21   20   19

6   5   4   3   2   1

AT LOVE GOD GREATLY, YOU'LL FIND REAL, AUTHENTIC WOMEN. WOMEN WHO ARE IMPERFECT, YET FORGIVEN.

Women who desire less of us, and a whole lot more of Jesus. Women who long to know God through His Word, because we know that Truth transforms and sets us free. Women who are better together, saturated in God's Word and in community with one another.

Welcome, friend. We're so glad you're here...

CONTENTS

WELCOME

We are glad you have decided to join us in this Bible study! First of all, please know that you have been prayed for! It is not a coincidence you are participating in this study.

Our prayer for you is simple: that you will grow closer to our Lord as you dig into His Word each and every day! As you develop the discipline of being in God's Word on a daily basis, our prayer is that you will fall in love with Him even more as you spend time reading from the Bible.

Each day before you read the assigned Scripture(s), pray and ask God to help you understand it. Invite Him to speak to you through His Word. Then listen. It's His job to speak to you, and it's your job to listen and obey.

Take time to read the verses over and over again. We are told in Proverbs to search and you will find: "Search for it like silver, and hunt for it like hidden treasure. Then you will understand" (Prov. 2:4–5 NCV).

All of us here at Love God Greatly can't wait for you to get started, and we hope to see you at the finish line. Endure, persevere, press on—and don't give up! Finish well what you are beginning today. We will be here every step of the way, cheering you on! We are in this together. Fight to rise early, to push back the stress of the day, to sit alone and spend time in God's Word! Let's see what God has in store for you in this study! Journey with us as we learn to love God greatly with our lives!

As you go through this study, join us in the following resources below:

Weekly Blog Posts •

Weekly Memory Verses •

Weekly Challenges •

Facebook, Twitter, Instagram •

LoveGodGreatly.com •

Hashtags: #LoveGodGreatly •

RESOURCES

Join Us

ONLINE

lovegodgreatly.com

STORE

lovegodgreatly.com/store

FACEBOOK

facebook.com/LoveGodGreatly

INSTAGRAM

instagram.com/lovegodgreatlyofficial

TWITTER

@_LoveGodGreatly

DOWNLOAD THE APP

CONTACT US

info@lovegodgreatly.com

CONNECT

#LoveGodGreatly

LOVE
GOD
GREATLY

Love God Greatly (LGG) is a beautiful community of women who use a variety of technology platforms to keep each other accountable in God's Word. We start with a simple Bible reading plan, but it doesn't stop there.

Some women gather in homes and churches locally, while others connect online with women across the globe. Whatever the method, we lovingly lock arms and unite for this purpose: to love God greatly with our lives.

In today's fast-paced technology-driven world, it would be easy to study God's Word in an isolated environment that lacks encouragement or support, but that isn't the intention here at Love God Greatly. God created us to live in community with Him and with those around us.

Would you consider reaching out and doing this study with someone?

We need each other, and we live life better together. Because of this, would you consider reaching out and doing this study with someone?

Rest assured we'll be studying right alongside you—learning with you, cheering for you, enjoying sweet fellowship, and smiling from ear to ear as we watch God unite women together—intentionally connecting hearts and minds for His glory.

So here's the challenge: call your mom, your sister, your grandma, the girl across the street, or the college friend across the country. Gather a group of girls from your church or workplace, or meet in a coffee shop with friends you have always wished you knew better.

Arm-in-arm and hand-in-hand, let's do this thing...together.

SOAP STUDY
HOW AND WHY TO SOAP

In this study we offer you a study journal to accompany the verses we are reading. This journal is designed to help you interact with God's Word and learn to dig deeper, encouraging you to slow down and reflect on what God is saying to you that day.

At Love God Greatly, we use the SOAP Bible study method. Before beginning, let's take a moment to define this method and share why we recommend using it during your quiet time in the following pages.

The most important ingredients in the SOAP method are your interaction with God's Word and your application of His Word to your life.

It's one thing to simply read Scripture. But when you interact with it, intentionally slowing down to really reflect on it, suddenly words start popping off the page. The SOAP method allows you to dig deeper into Scripture and see more than you would if you simply read the verses and then went on your merry way.

The most important ingredients in the SOAP method are your interaction with God's Word and your application of His Word to your life:

Blessed is the one who does not walk in step with the wicked or stand in the way that sinners take or sit in the company of mockers, but whose delight is in the law of the LORD, and who meditates on his law day and night. That person is like a tree planted by streams of water, which yields its fruit in season and whose leaf does not wither—whatever they do prospers. (Ps. 1:1–3, NIV)

Please take the time to SOAP through our Bible studies and see for yourself how much more you get from your daily reading.

You'll be amazed.

SOAP STUDY (CONTINUED)
WHAT DOES SOAP MEAN?

S STANDS FOR
SCRIPTURE

Physically write out the verses.

You'll be amazed at what God will reveal to you just by taking the time to slow down and write out what you are reading!

MONDAY

READ
Colossians 1:5–8

SOAP
Colossians 1:5–8

Scripture

WRITE
OUT THE
SCRIPTURE
PASSAGE
FOR THE
DAY.

The faith and love that spring from the hope stored up for you in heaven and about which you have already heard in the true message of the gospel that has come to you. In the same way, the gospel is bearing fruit and growing throughout the whole world just as it has been doing among you since the day you heard it and truly understood God's grace. You learned it from Epaphras our dear fellow servant, who is a faithful minister of Christ on our behalf, and who also told us of your love in the Spirit.

Observations

WRITE
DOWN 1 OR 2
OBSERVATIONS
FROM THE
PASSAGE.

When you combine faith and love, you get hope. We must remember that our hope is in heaven; it is yet to come. The gospel is the Word of truth. This gospel is continually bearing fruit and growing from the first day to the last. It just takes one person to change a whole community. Epaphras.

O STANDS FOR
OBSERVATION

What do you see in the verses that you're reading?

Who is the intended audience? Is there a repetition of words?

What words stand out to you?

A STANDS FOR APPLICATION

This is when God's Word becomes personal.

What is God saying to you today?

How can you apply what you just read to your own personal life?

What changes do you need to make? Is there action you need to take?

Applications

WRITE DOWN 1 OR 2 APPLICATIONS FROM THE PASSAGE.

God used one man, Epaphras, to change a whole town. I was reminded that we are simply called to tell others about Christ; it's God's job to spread the gospel, to grow it, and have it bear fruit. I felt today's verses were almost directly spoken to Love God Greatly women: The gospel is bearing fruit and growing throughout the whole world just as it has been doing among you since the day you heard it and truly understood God's grace.

Pray

WRITE OUT A PRAYER OVER WHAT YOU LEARNED FROM TODAY'S PASSAGE.

Dear Lord, please help me to be an Epaphras, to tell others about You and then leave the results in Your loving hands. Please help me to understand and apply personally what I have read today to my life, thereby becoming more and more like You each and every day. Help me to live a life that bears the fruit of faith and love, anchoring my hope in heaven, not here on earth. Help me to remember that the best is yet to come!

P STANDS FOR PRAYER

Pray God's Word back to Him. Spend time thanking Him.

If He has revealed something to you during this time in His Word, pray about it.

If He has revealed some sin that is in your life, confess. And remember, He loves you dearly.

A RECIPE
FOR YOU
FRUIT DUMPLINGS

Ingredients

2 lbs Potatoes

¾ cup Semolina

1 cup All-Purpose Flour

2 Eggs

Salt

Fruit

You can add any fruit of your choice to these dough balls, such as berries (strawberry, raspberry, blueberry), apricots, or plums.

Directions

- Place potatoes in a large pan of boiling water and boil for 20 minutes. Let potatoes cool down before peeling off their skin and grate using a cheese grater.

- Mix grated potatoes with semolina, flour, eggs and a pinch of salt until the dough is well mixed and sticky.

- Use additional flour to cover a worktop surface and roll dough into a log shape. The dough will stick to your fingers, so add additional flour as needed.

- Cut the dough into small pieces, about 1-1.5 inches long, depending on the size dough balls you like.

- Take each piece and flatten with your fingers to create a circle, place a piece of fruit of your choice on top (see notes) and roll up to a ball with fruit in the middle.

- When you have used up all dough, bring a large pan of water (with a pinch of salt) to boil and add 5-10 dough balls at a time, depending on the size of your pan. The dough balls are cooked when they come up to the surface.

- Serve with icing sugar, hot cocoa powder and melted butter on top!

LGG CZECH TESTIMONIES

KRISTÝNA ČIHÁKOVÁ, CZECH REPUBLIC

I have gradually fallen in love with God's Word.

I first heard about Love God Greatly from a friend when I was looking for a way to regularly read the Bible, while somehow keeping a written record of what God has been showing me. I prayed about it for a little while and then Misa approached me at youth group to tell me about the Psalm 119 study. She invited me to join her online study group.

I have really enjoyed reading through these studies. It's a joy and encouragement every step of the way. In the morning, I record what God is showing me through the Bible, and then I am further encouraged through the Facebook posts and blog articles of LGG. I like that LGG emphasizes God's mercy, love, and forgiveness. Even though our God is truly like that, I often forget, so I am thankful to be reminded through my study group or through the blog.

Thanks to LGG I have gradually fallen in love with God's Word. I tried to read regularly before as well, but it has become a joy now instead of an obligation. Thanks be to Jesus for that! I'm also so thankful that, through one of these study groups, I got to know my now beloved roommate at University.

PETRA STONEMAN, NORTHERN IRELAND

I started translating for Love God Greatly a year after I became a Christian – with no experience, little theology, and a whole lot of burning passion to bring something beautiful and resourceful to the women in my country.

Originally from the Czech Republic, I was living in Northern Ireland as a church youth intern at the age of 19. Being part of a local church in Czech before that made me aware of how little church leaders had to work with when it came to

group study resources – however, I also fondly remember how what they lacked in recourses they made up with passion and determination to serve their people well.

When I moved to Northern Ireland initially for one year, I could not believe the resources, types of Bibles, study guides AND Christian literature available in English - both in store and especially online!

I wanted it.

I wanted it for myself, I wanted it for my small group at home, I also wanted it for the Czech women all around the country! I longed to make their devotional time more beautiful and joyful through quality resources that would be easily accessible – and with Love God Greatly, this also meant free!

God has provided a sweet community of women... who encourage, inspire, and motivate me to spend time in God's Word every day...

Over the many years of being part of the LGG ministry, I have come to appreciate God's Word in new ways. God has provided a sweet community of women – translators and leaders – who encourage, inspire, and motivate me to spend time in God's Word every day, and who live out the difference this makes in their lives. I have also gained a rich wealth of knowledge from translating LGG resources into the Czech language – each document, paragraph, and word has been prayed over as I typed, deleted, pondered, and re-typed. And it has led me to a deeper relationship with our loving Father because I realize that I cannot encourage and lead others in their study of the Scriptures unless I am doing the same. I have, therefore, – imperfectly still – learned the sweet discipline of soaking in passages of the Bible and memorizing verses daily.

Never would I have imagined this wild adventure God would take me on by saying a loud, passionate YES... the resonant YES of a new believer, with the kind of passion that would slowly dissolve and eventually turn into a deep fire burning for His people and His kingdom. If He can use someone like me, He sure can use someone like you!

To connect with LGG Czech Branch:

- milujbohanesmirne.blog
- facebook.com/MilujBohaNesmirne

Do you know someone who could use our *Love God Greatly* Bible studies in Czech? If so, make sure and tell them about LGG Czech and all the amazing Bible study resources we provide to help equip them with God's Word!!!

WALKING IN VICTORY

A study on Joshua

Let's Begin

INTRODUCTION
WALKING IN VICTORY

Some of us live our lives fearing the future. We live in the "what ifs" instead of focusing on the things God has already given us. We have an inheritance in Christ that nobody can take away from us. We have been promised an abundant life but we´re living on crumbs. Why? Because we don´t realize that we are fighting this battle named "life" from a position of victory.

The book of Joshua teaches us to remember the promises God has given us and to trust God in everything He assigns to us. Joshua shows us how to walk in victory.

When Moses dies right before the people of Israel cross the Jordan, Joshua is given the task of leading the people to the Promised Land. He didn´t have time to consider whether he wants the job or if he felt prepared for the task. He received a command from God and he obeyed.

God sent Joshua with the promise that He had already given Israel the land of Canaan (Joshua 1:2). And he crossed the Jordan claiming that promise, trusting that God would be with him every step of the way and that He wouldn´t forsake him.

The promise of the land of Canaan has its origin in God's promise to Abraham (Genesis 12:1–3). God called Abraham from among the nations and gave him several promises, including land, a nation, and blessing to the rest of the nations through him. The story of Joshua develops each of these promises, but the focus and emphasis are clearly on God's promise of land.

"The LORD gave to Israel all the land that he swore to give to their fathers. And they took possession of it, and they settled there." (Joshua 21:43)

After forty years of wandering in the wilderness, Israel claimed their inheritance and enjoyed the blessings of the land that God had prepared for them.

The land was already theirs. However, there were some things Joshua had to do:

Joshua had to be brave and courageous.
Joshua had to be careful to live God´s Word.
Joshua had to meditate in God´s Word day and night.
Joshua had to trust God´s promises.

Walking in victory relies on God´s promises but it´s not passive. It requires action from us to embrace those promises and live in them every day. Israel owned the land because of God's gracious covenant with Abraham (Genesis 12:1–5), but their enjoyment of the land depended on their faithful obedience to God.

The same God who was with Joshua and the Israelites is with us today. He has given us the same promises and He wants us to claim our inheritance. We pray this study helps you to start walking in victory!

READING PLAN

WEEK 1

Monday – Be in God's Word Every Day
READ: Joshua 1:5-9
SOAP: Joshua 1:8
   For further reading – Joshua 1:10-18

Tuesday – Unexpected Help
READ: Joshua 2:1-7; Hebrews 11:31
SOAP: Hebrews 11:31
   For further reading – Joshua 2:8-14

Wednesday – Claim All God Has Already Given You
READ: Joshua 2:15-18; 24; Exodus 23:31
SOAP: Joshua 2:24
   For further reading – Joshua 2:19-23

Thursday – Be Holy
READ: Joshua 3:1-6; Leviticus 20:7; 1 Peter 1:16
SOAP: Joshua 3:5
   For further reading – Joshua 3:7-17

Friday – Remember the Things God Has Made for You
READ: Joshua 4:1-7; Psalm 78:2-4; Psalm 44:1
SOAP: Joshua 4:6-7; Psalm 44:1
   For further reading – Joshua 4:8-14

WEEK 2

Monday – We Have a Mighty God
READ: Joshua 4:19-24; 1 Kings 8:41-43
SOAP: Joshua 4:23-24
   For further reading – Joshua 4:15-18

Tuesday – A Pact is Renewed with the New Generation
READ: Joshua 5:2-9; Genesis 17:9-10; Psalm 105:8-11
SOAP: Psalm 105:8
   For further reading – Joshua 5:1; 10-15

Wednesday – You Fight from Victory, Not for Victory
READ: Joshua 6:2-6; Romans 8:31
SOAP: Romans 8:31
   For further reading – Joshua 6:1; 7-13

Thursday – Victory in Jericho
READ: Joshua 6:14-17; 20; 27
SOAP: Joshua 6:27
   For further reading – Joshua 6:18-27

Friday – Consequences of Sin
READ: Joshua 7:1; 11-14; Romans 6:23
SOAP: Joshua 7:11; Romans 6:23
   For further reading – Joshua 7:2-10

WEEK 3

Monday – Confession of Sins
READ: Joshua 7:16-21; Proverbs 28:13
SOAP: Proverbs 28:13
For further reading – Joshua 7:15; 22-26

Tuesday – Do Everything According to the Commandments of the Lord
READ: Joshua 8:1-10; 1 Samuel 15:22
SOAP: 1 Samuel 15:22
For further reading – Joshua 8:11-17

Wednesday – God Gives Us Victory
READ: Joshua 8:18-22; 1 Corinthians 15:57
SOAP: 1 Corinthians 15:57
For further reading – Joshua 8:23-29

Thursday – Listen to God's Word
READ: Joshua 8:30-35; Deuteronomy 28:1-2
SOAP: Deuteronomy 28:1-2

Friday – The Results of Not Consulting with the Lord
READ: Joshua 9:1-6; 14-15; Psalm 33:10-11
SOAP: Psalm 33:10-11
For further reading – Joshua 9:7-13

WEEK 4

Monday – Wrong Allies
READ: Joshua 9:22-27; Psalm 19:12-13
SOAP: Psalm 19:12-13
For further reading – Joshua 9:16-27

Tuesday – Victory in Prayer
READ: Joshua 10:12-14; 20-21
SOAP: Joshua 10:14
For further reading – Joshua 10:1-11; 15-19

Wednesday – God Fights for You
READ: Joshua 10:38-43; Jeremiah 1:19
SOAP: Jeremiah 1:19
For further reading – Joshua 10:22-37

Thursday – Small Army, Big Victory
READ: Joshua 11:3-10; 2 Kings 6:16-17
SOAP: 2 Kings 6:16
For further reading – Joshua 11:1-2; 11-23

Friday – Bad Choices
READ: Joshua 13:1-8; Isaiah 66:3-4
SOAP: Isaiah 66:3-4
For further reading – Joshua 12; 13:9-33

WEEK 5

Monday – Give Me That Mountain
READ: Joshua 14:6-13
SOAP: Joshua 14:12
  For further reading – Joshua 14:1-5; 14-15; Joshua 15

Tuesday – The Problem of the Ego
READ: Joshua 17:12-18; 1 Corinthians 5:6-8; James 4:16
SOAP: 1 Corinthians 5:6-8
  For further reading – Joshua 16; 17:1-11

Wednesday – Spiritual Slack
READ: Joshua 18:1-10; Proverbs 10:4
SOAP: Proverbs 10:4
  For further reading – Joshua 18:11-28; Joshua 19

Thursday – God is our Refuge
READ: Joshua 20:1-6; Hebrews 6:18; Psalm 94:21-22
SOAP: Psalm 94:22
  For further reading – Joshua 20:7-9

Friday – Spiritual Influence of the Levites
READ: Joshua 21:1-3; 2 Chronicles 17:7-9; Nehemiah 8:7-8; Psalm 119:27
SOAP: Psalm 119:27
  For further reading – Joshua 21:4-12

WEEK 6

Monday - God Fulfills His Promises
READ: Joshua 21:43-45
SOAP: Joshua 21:45
  For further reading – Joshua 21:13-42

Tuesday – Your Spiritual Responsibility
READ: Joshua 22:1-6; Matthew 22:36-38; John 14:15
SOAP: John 14:15
  For further reading – Joshua 22:7-34

Wednesday – Be Strong to Keep God's Word
READ: Joshua 23:6-12
SOAP: Joshua 23:8
  For further reading – Joshua 23:1-5; 13-16

Thursday – Choose Whom You Will Serve
READ: Joshua 24:11-15
SOAP: Joshua 24:15
  For further reading – Joshua 24:1-10

Friday – Vessels for Honorable Use
READ: Joshua 24:19-23; 2 Timothy 2:20-21
SOAP: 2 Timothy 2:21
  For further reading – Joshua 24:16-18; 24-33

YOUR
GOALS

We believe it's important to write out goals for this study. Take some time now and write three goals you would like to focus on as you begin to rise each day and dig into God's Word. Make sure and refer back to these goals throughout the next weeks to help you stay focused. You can do it!

1.

2.

3.

Signature:

Date:

WEEK 1

Have I not commanded you?
Be strong and courageous.
Do not be frightened, and do not be
dismayed, for the Lord your God
is with you wherever you go.

JOSHUA 1:9

PRAYER

Prayer focus for this week:
Spend time praying for your family members.

MONDAY

TUESDAY

WEDNESDAY

THURSDAY

FRIDAY

CHALLENGE
You can find this listed in our Monday blog post.

26

MONDAY
Scripture for Week 1

Joshua 1:5-9

5 No man shall be able to stand before you all the days of your life. Just as I was with Moses, so I will be with you. I will not leave you or forsake you. 6 Be strong and courageous, for you shall cause this people to inherit the land that I swore to their fathers to give them. 7 Only be strong and very courageous, being careful to do according to all the law that Moses my servant commanded you. Do not turn from it to the right hand or to the left, that you may have good success wherever you go. 8 This Book of the Law shall not depart from your mouth, but you shall meditate on it day and night, so that you may be careful to do according to all that is written in it. For then you will make your way prosperous, and then you will have good success. 9 Have I not commanded you? Be strong and courageous. Do not be frightened, and do not be dismayed, for the Lord your God is with you wherever you go."

MONDAY

READ:
Joshua 1:5-9

SOAP:
Joshua 1:8

Scripture

WRITE
OUT THE
SCRIPTURE
PASSAGE
FOR THE
DAY.

Observations

WRITE
DOWN 1 OR 2
OBSERVATIONS
FROM THE
PASSAGE.

Applications

WRITE
DOWN 1 OR 2
APPLICATIONS
FROM THE
PASSAGE.

Pray

WRITE OUT
A PRAYER
OVER WHAT
YOU LEARNED
FROM TODAY'S
PASSAGE.

TUESDAY
Scripture for Week 1

Joshua 2:1-7

1 And Joshua the son of Nun sent two men secretly from Shittim as spies, saying, "Go, view the land, especially Jericho." And they went and came into the house of a prostitute whose name was Rahab and lodged there. 2 And it was told to the king of Jericho, "Behold, men of Israel have come here tonight to search out the land." 3 Then the king of Jericho sent to Rahab, saying, "Bring out the men who have come to you, who entered your house, for they have come to search out all the land." 4 But the woman had taken the two men and hidden them. And she said, "True, the men came to me, but I did not know where they were from. 5 And when the gate was about to be closed at dark, the men went out. I do not know where the men went. Pursue them quickly, for you will overtake them." 6 But she had brought them up to the roof and hid them with the stalks of flax that she had laid in order on the roof. 7 So the men pursued after them on the way to the Jordan as far as the fords. And the gate was shut as soon as the pursuers had gone out.

Hebrews 11:31

31 By faith Rahab the prostitute did not perish with those who were disobedient, because she had given a friendly welcome to the spies.

TUESDAY

READ:
Joshua 2:1-7; Hebrews 11:31

SOAP:
Hebrews 11:31

Scripture

WRITE
OUT THE
SCRIPTURE
PASSAGE
FOR THE
DAY.

Observations

WRITE
DOWN 1 OR 2
OBSERVATIONS
FROM THE
PASSAGE.

Applications

WRITE
DOWN 1 OR 2
APPLICATIONS
FROM THE
PASSAGE.

Pray

WRITE OUT
A PRAYER
OVER WHAT
YOU LEARNED
FROM TODAY'S
PASSAGE.

WEDNESDAY
Scripture for Week 1

Joshua 2:15-18; 24

15 Then she let them down by a rope through the window, for her house was built into the city wall, so that she lived in the wall. 16 And she said to them, "Go into the hills, or the pursuers will encounter you, and hide there three days until the pursuers have returned. Then afterward you may go your way." 17 The men said to her, "We will be guiltless with respect to this oath of yours that you have made us swear. 18 Behold, when we come into the land, you shall tie this scarlet cord in the window through which you let us down, and you shall gather into your house your father and mother, your brothers, and all your father's household.

24 And they said to Joshua, "Truly the Lord has given all the land into our hands. And also, all the inhabitants of the land melt away because of us."

Exodus 23:31

31 And I will set your border from the Red Sea to the Sea of the Philistines, and from the wilderness to the Euphrates, for I will give the inhabitants of the land into your hand, and you shall drive them out before you.

WEDNESDAY

READ:
Joshua 2:15-18; 24; Exodus 23:31

SOAP:
Joshua 2:24

Scripture

WRITE
OUT THE
SCRIPTURE
PASSAGE
FOR THE
DAY.

Observations

WRITE
DOWN 1 OR 2
OBSERVATIONS
FROM THE
PASSAGE.

Applications

WRITE
DOWN 1 OR 2
APPLICATIONS
FROM THE
PASSAGE.

Pray

WRITE OUT
A PRAYER
OVER WHAT
YOU LEARNED
FROM TODAY'S
PASSAGE.

THURSDAY

Scripture for Week 1

Joshua 3:1-6

1 Then Joshua rose early in the morning and they set out from Shittim. And they came to the Jordan, he and all the people of Israel, and lodged there before they passed over. 2 At the end of three days the officers went through the camp 3 and commanded the people, "As soon as you see the ark of the covenant of the Lordyour God being carried by the Levitical priests, then you shall set out from your place and follow it. 4 Yet there shall be a distance between you and it, about 2,000 cubits in length. Do not come near it, in order that you may know the way you shall go, for you have not passed this way before." 5 Then Joshua said to the people, "Consecrate yourselves, for tomorrow the Lord will do wonders among you." 6 And Joshua said to the priests, "Take up the ark of the covenant and pass on before the people." So they took up the ark of the covenant and went before the people.

Leviticus 20:7

7 Consecrate yourselves, therefore, and be holy, for I am the Lord your God.

1 Peter 1:16

16 since it is written, "You shall be holy, for I am holy."

THURSDAY

READ:
Joshua 3:1-6; Leviticus 20:7; 1 Peter 1:16

SOAP:
Joshua 3:5

Scripture

WRITE
OUT THE
SCRIPTURE
PASSAGE
FOR THE
DAY.

Observations

WRITE
DOWN 1 OR 2
OBSERVATIONS
FROM THE
PASSAGE.

Applications

WRITE
DOWN 1 OR 2
APPLICATIONS
FROM THE
PASSAGE.

Pray

WRITE OUT
A PRAYER
OVER WHAT
YOU LEARNED
FROM TODAY'S
PASSAGE.

FRIDAY
Scripture for Week 1

Joshua 4:1-7
1 When all the nation had finished passing over the Jordan,
the Lord said to Joshua, 2 "Take twelve men from the people, from
each tribe a man, 3 and command them, saying, 'Take twelve stones
from here out of the midst of the Jordan, from the very place where
the priests' feet stood firmly, and bring them over with you and
lay them down in the place where you lodge tonight.'" 4 Then
Joshua called the twelve men from the people of Israel, whom he
had appointed, a man from each tribe. 5 And Joshua said to them,
"Pass on before the ark of the Lord your God into the midst of
the Jordan, and take up each of you a stone upon his shoulder,
according to the number of the tribes of the people of Israel, 6 that
this may be a sign among you. When your children ask in time to
come, 'What do those stones mean to you?' 7 then you shall tell
them that the waters of the Jordan were cut off before the ark of the
covenant of the Lord. When it passed over the Jordan, the waters
of the Jordan were cut off. So these stones shall be to the people of
Israel a memorial forever."

Psalm 78:2-4
2 I will open my mouth in a parable;
    I will utter dark sayings from of old,
3 things that we have heard and known,
    that our fathers have told us.
4 We will not hide them from their children,
    but tell to the coming generation
the glorious deeds of the Lord, and his might,
    and the wonders that he has done.

Psalm 44:1
1 O God, we have heard with our ears,
    our fathers have told us,
what deeds you performed in their days,
    in the days of old:

FRIDAY

READ:
Joshua 4:1-7; Psalm 78:2-4; Psalm 44:1

SOAP:
Joshua 4:6-7; Psalm 44:1

Scripture

WRITE
OUT THE
SCRIPTURE
PASSAGE
FOR THE
DAY.

Observations

WRITE
DOWN 1 OR 2
OBSERVATIONS
FROM THE
PASSAGE.

Applications

WRITE
DOWN 1 OR 2
APPLICATIONS
FROM THE
PASSAGE.

Pray

WRITE OUT
A PRAYER
OVER WHAT
YOU LEARNED
FROM TODAY'S
PASSAGE.

REFLECTION
QUESTIONS

1. What keeps you from being in God's Word every day? How can you overcome that?

2. Are you living for God with boldness? Why or why not?

3. Do you doubt the things God is asking you to do? Are you limiting His power instead of trusting Him?

4. What does "holy" mean? How can we be holy in our daily lives?

5. Why does remembering the things God has created for us and His answers to our prayers give us encouragement?

NOTES

WEEK 2

He remembers his covenant forever,

the word that he commanded,

for a thousand generations

PSALM 105:8

PRAYER

WRITE DOWN YOUR PRAYER REQUESTS
AND PRAISES FOR EACH DAY.

Prayer focus for this week:
Spend time praying for your country.

MONDAY

TUESDAY

WEDNESDAY

THURSDAY

FRIDAY

CHALLENGE

You can find this listed in our Monday blog post.

MONDAY
Scripture for Week 2

Joshua 4:19-24

19 The people came up out of the Jordan on the tenth day of the first month, and they encamped at Gilgal on the east border of Jericho. 20 And those twelve stones, which they took out of the Jordan, Joshua set up at Gilgal. 21 And he said to the people of Israel, "When your children ask their fathers in times to come, 'What do these stones mean?' 22 then you shall let your children know, 'Israel passed over this Jordan on dry ground.' 23 For the Lord your God dried up the waters of the Jordan for you until you passed over, as the Lord your God did to the Red Sea, which he dried up for us until we passed over, 24 so that all the peoples of the earth may know that the hand of the Lord is mighty, that you may fear the Lordyour God forever."

1 Kings 8:41-43

41 "Likewise, when a foreigner, who is not of your people Israel, comes from a far country for your name's sake 42 (for they shall hear of your great name and your mighty hand, and of your outstretched arm), when he comes and prays toward this house, 43 hear in heaven your dwelling place and do according to all for which the foreigner calls to you, in order that all the peoples of the earth may know your name and fear you, as do your people Israel, and that they may know that this house that I have built is called by your name.

MONDAY

READ:
Joshua 4:19-24; 1 Kings 8:41-43

SOAP:
Joshua 4:23-24

Scripture

WRITE
OUT THE
SCRIPTURE
PASSAGE
FOR THE
DAY.

Observations

WRITE
DOWN 1 OR 2
OBSERVATIONS
FROM THE
PASSAGE.

Applications

WRITE
DOWN 1 OR 2
APPLICATIONS
FROM THE
PASSAGE.

Pray

WRITE OUT
A PRAYER
OVER WHAT
YOU LEARNED
FROM TODAY'S
PASSAGE.

TUESDAY
Scripture for Week 2

Joshua 5:2-9
2 At that time the Lord said to Joshua, "Make flint knives and circumcise the sons of Israel a second time." 3 So Joshua made flint knives and circumcised the sons of Israel at Gibeath-haaraloth. 4 And this is the reason why Joshua circumcised them: all the males of the people who came out of Egypt, all the men of war, had died in the wilderness on the way after they had come out of Egypt. 5 Though all the people who came out had been circumcised, yet all the people who were born on the way in the wilderness after they had come out of Egypt had not been circumcised. 6 For the people of Israel walked forty years in the wilderness, until all the nation, the men of war who came out of Egypt, perished, because they did not obey the voice of the Lord; the Lord swore to them that he would not let them see the land that the Lord had sworn to their fathers to give to us, a land flowing with milk and honey. 7 So it was their children, whom he raised up in their place, that Joshua circumcised. For they were uncircumcised, because they had not been circumcised on the way.

8 When the circumcising of the whole nation was finished, they remained in their places in the camp until they were healed. 9 And the Lord said to Joshua, "Today I have rolled away the reproach of Egypt from you." And so the name of that place is called Gilgal to this day.

Genesis 17:9-10
9 And God said to Abraham, "As for you, you shall keep my covenant, you and your offspring after you throughout their generations. 10 This is my covenant, which you shall keep, between me and you and your offspring after you: Every male among you shall be circumcised.

Psalm 105:8-11
8 He remembers his covenant forever,
   the word that he commanded, for a thousand generations,
9 the covenant that he made with Abraham,
   his sworn promise to Isaac,
10 which he confirmed to Jacob as a statute,
   to Israel as an everlasting covenant,
11 saying, "To you I will give the land of Canaan
   as your portion for an inheritance."

TUESDAY

READ:
Joshua 5:2-9; Genesis 17:9-10; Psalm 105:8-11

SOAP:
Psalm 105:8

Scripture

WRITE
OUT THE
SCRIPTURE
PASSAGE
FOR THE
DAY.

Observations

WRITE
DOWN 1 OR 2
OBSERVATIONS
FROM THE
PASSAGE.

Applications

WRITE
DOWN 1 OR 2
APPLICATIONS
FROM THE
PASSAGE.

Pray

WRITE OUT
A PRAYER
OVER WHAT
YOU LEARNED
FROM TODAY'S
PASSAGE.

WEDNESDAY

Scripture for Week 2

Joshua 6:2-6

2 And the Lord said to Joshua, "See, I have given Jericho into your hand, with its king and mighty men of valor. 3 You shall march around the city, all the men of war going around the city once. Thus shall you do for six days. 4 Seven priests shall bear seven trumpets of rams' horns before the ark. On the seventh day you shall march around the city seven times, and the priests shall blow the trumpets. 5 And when they make a long blast with the ram's horn, when you hear the sound of the trumpet, then all the people shall shout with a great shout, and the wall of the city will fall down flat, and the people shall go up, everyone straight before him." 6 So Joshua the son of Nun called the priests and said to them, "Take up the ark of the covenant and let seven priests bear seven trumpets of rams' horns before the ark of the Lord."

Romans 8:31

31 What then shall we say to these things? If God is for us, who can be against us?

WEDNESDAY

READ:
Joshua 6:2-6; Romans 8:31

SOAP:
Romans 8:31

Scripture

WRITE
OUT THE
SCRIPTURE
PASSAGE
FOR THE
DAY.

Observations

WRITE
DOWN 1 OR 2
OBSERVATIONS
FROM THE
PASSAGE.

Applications

WRITE
DOWN 1 OR 2
APPLICATIONS
FROM THE
PASSAGE.

Pray

WRITE OUT
A PRAYER
OVER WHAT
YOU LEARNED
FROM TODAY'S
PASSAGE.

THURSDAY
Scripture for Week 2

Joshua 6:14-17; 20; 27

14 And the second day they marched around the city once, and returned into the camp. So they did for six days.

15 On the seventh day they rose early, at the dawn of day, and marched around the city in the same manner seven times. It was only on that day that they marched around the city seven times. 16 And at the seventh time, when the priests had blown the trumpets, Joshua said to the people, "Shout, for the Lord has given you the city. 17 And the city and all that is within it shall be devoted to the Lord for destruction. Only Rahab the prostitute and all who are with her in her house shall live, because she hid the messengers whom we sent.

20 So the people shouted, and the trumpets were blown. As soon as the people heard the sound of the trumpet, the people shouted a great shout, and the wall fell down flat, so that the people went up into the city, every man straight before him, and they captured the city.

27 So the Lord was with Joshua, and his fame was in all the land.

THURSDAY

READ:
Joshua 6:14-17; 20; 27

SOAP:
Joshua 6:27

Scripture

WRITE
OUT THE
SCRIPTURE
PASSAGE
FOR THE
DAY.

Observations

WRITE
DOWN 1 OR 2
OBSERVATIONS
FROM THE
PASSAGE.

Applications

WRITE
DOWN 1 OR 2
APPLICATIONS
FROM THE
PASSAGE.

Pray

WRITE OUT
A PRAYER
OVER WHAT
YOU LEARNED
FROM TODAY'S
PASSAGE.

FRIDAY
Scripture for Week 2

Joshua 7:1; 11-14
1 But the people of Israel broke faith in regard to the devoted things, for Achan the son of Carmi, son of Zabdi, son of Zerah, of the tribe of Judah, took some of the devoted things. And the anger of the Lord burned against the people of Israel.

11 Israel has sinned; they have transgressed my covenant that I commanded them; they have taken some of the devoted things; they have stolen and lied and put them among their own belongings. 12 Therefore the people of Israel cannot stand before their enemies. They turn their backs before their enemies, because they have become devoted for destruction. I will be with you no more, unless you destroy the devoted things from among you. 13 Get up! Consecrate the people and say, 'Consecrate yourselves for tomorrow; for thus says the Lord, God of Israel, "There are devoted things in your midst, O Israel. You cannot stand before your enemies until you take away the devoted things from among you." 14 In the morning therefore you shall be brought near by your tribes. And the tribe that the Lord takes by lot shall come near by clans. And the clan that the Lord takes shall come near by households. And the household that the Lord takes shall come near man by man.

Romans 6:23
23 For the wages of sin is death, but the free gift of God is eternal life in Christ Jesus our Lord.

FRIDAY

READ:
Joshua 7:1; 11-14; Romans 6:23

SOAP:
Joshua 7:11; Romans 6:23

Scripture

WRITE
OUT THE
SCRIPTURE
PASSAGE
FOR THE
DAY.

Observations

WRITE
DOWN 1 OR 2
OBSERVATIONS
FROM THE
PASSAGE.

Applications

WRITE
DOWN 1 OR 2
APPLICATIONS
FROM THE
PASSAGE.

Pray

WRITE OUT
A PRAYER
OVER WHAT
YOU LEARNED
FROM TODAY'S
PASSAGE.

REFLECTION
QUESTIONS

1. How does knowing the mighty things God has done for His people encourage you to face your life?

2. Circumcision was the first act of preparation to conquer the land. What does circumcision represent? How is it connected to us today? (Read Philippians 3:3; Colossians 2:11)

3. What struggles are you facing today? How can Romans 8:31 encourage you to fight? Read Psalm 27 and take heart, God is with you.

4. What would you have thought if God had commanded you to march around Jericho? What do you do when He commands you to do things you don't understand?

5. Sin always has consequences. How does Romans 6:23 encourage you today?

NOTES

WEEK 3

But thanks be to God, who gives us the victory through our Lord Jesus Christ.

1 CORINTHIANS 15:57

PRAYER

Prayer focus for this week:
Spend time praying for your friends.

MONDAY

TUESDAY

WEDNESDAY

THURSDAY

FRIDAY

CHALLENGE

You can find this listed in our Monday blog post.

MONDAY

Scripture for Week 3

Joshua 7:16-21

16 So Joshua rose early in the morning and brought Israel near tribe
by tribe, and the tribe of Judah was taken. 17 And he brought near
the clans of Judah, and the clan of the Zerahites was taken. And
he brought near the clan of the Zerahites man by man, and Zabdi
was taken. 18 And he brought near his household man by man, and
Achan the son of Carmi, son of Zabdi, son of Zerah, of the tribe
of Judah, was taken. 19 Then Joshua said to Achan, "My son, give
glory to the LordGod of Israel and give praise to him. And tell me
now what you have done; do not hide it from me." 20 And Achan
answered Joshua, "Truly I have sinned against the Lord God of
Israel, and this is what I did: 21 when I saw among the spoil a
beautiful cloak from Shinar, and 200 shekels of silver, and a bar
of gold weighing 50 shekels, then I coveted them and took them.
And see, they are hidden in the earth inside my tent, with the silver
underneath."

Proverbs 28:13

13 Whoever conceals his transgressions will not prosper,
　　but he who confesses and forsakes them will obtain mercy.

MONDAY

READ:
Joshua 7:16-21; Proverbs 28:13

SOAP:
Proverbs 28:13

Scripture

WRITE
OUT THE
SCRIPTURE
PASSAGE
FOR THE
DAY.

Observations

WRITE
DOWN 1 OR 2
OBSERVATIONS
FROM THE
PASSAGE.

Applications

WRITE
DOWN 1 OR 2
APPLICATIONS
FROM THE
PASSAGE.

Pray

WRITE OUT
A PRAYER
OVER WHAT
YOU LEARNED
FROM TODAY'S
PASSAGE.

TUESDAY
Scripture for Week 3

Joshua 8:1-10

1 And the Lord said to Joshua, "Do not fear and do not be dismayed. Take all the fighting men with you, and arise, go up to Ai. See, I have given into your hand the king of Ai, and his people, his city, and his land. 2 And you shall do to Ai and its king as you did to Jericho and its king. Only its spoil and its livestock you shall take as plunder for yourselves. Lay an ambush against the city, behind it."

3 So Joshua and all the fighting men arose to go up to Ai. And Joshua chose 30,000 mighty men of valor and sent them out by night. 4 And he commanded them, "Behold, you shall lie in ambush against the city, behind it. Do not go very far from the city, but all of you remain ready. 5 And I and all the people who are with me will approach the city. And when they come out against us just as before, we shall flee before them. 6 And they will come out after us, until we have drawn them away from the city. For they will say, 'They are fleeing from us, just as before.' So we will flee before them. 7 Then you shall rise up from the ambush and seize the city, for the Lord your God will give it into your hand. 8 And as soon as you have taken the city, you shall set the city on fire. You shall do according to the word of the Lord. See, I have commanded you." 9 So Joshua sent them out. And they went to the place of ambush and lay between Bethel and Ai, to the west of Ai, but Joshua spent that night among the people.

10 Joshua arose early in the morning and mustered the people and went up, he and the elders of Israel, before the people to Ai.

1 Samuel 15:22

22 And Samuel said,
"Has the Lord as great delight in burnt offerings and sacrifices,
    as in obeying the voice of the Lord?
Behold, to obey is better than sacrifice,
    and to listen than the fat of rams.

TUESDAY

READ:
Joshua 8:1-10; 1 Samuel 15:22

SOAP:
1 Samuel 15:22

Scripture

WRITE
OUT THE
SCRIPTURE
PASSAGE
FOR THE
DAY.

Observations

WRITE
DOWN 1 OR 2
OBSERVATIONS
FROM THE
PASSAGE.

Applications

WRITE
DOWN 1 OR 2
APPLICATIONS
FROM THE
PASSAGE.

Pray

WRITE OUT
A PRAYER
OVER WHAT
YOU LEARNED
FROM TODAY'S
PASSAGE.

WEDNESDAY
Scripture for Week 3

Joshua 8:18-22

18 Then the Lord said to Joshua, "Stretch out the javelin that is in your hand toward Ai, for I will give it into your hand." And Joshua stretched out the javelin that was in his hand toward the city. 19 And the men in the ambush rose quickly out of their place, and as soon as he had stretched out his hand, they ran and entered the city and captured it. And they hurried to set the city on fire. 20 So when the men of Ai looked back, behold, the smoke of the city went up to heaven, and they had no power to flee this way or that, for the people who fled to the wilderness turned back against the pursuers. 21 And when Joshua and all Israel saw that the ambush had captured the city, and that the smoke of the city went up, then they turned back and struck down the men of Ai. 22 And the others came out from the city against them, so they were in the midst of Israel, some on this side, and some on that side. And Israel struck them down, until there was left none that survived or escaped.

1 Corinthians 15:57

57 But thanks be to God, who gives us the victory through our Lord Jesus Christ.

WEDNESDAY

READ:
Joshua 8:18-22; 1 Corinthians 15:57

SOAP:
1 Corinthians 15:57

Scripture

WRITE
OUT THE
SCRIPTURE
PASSAGE
FOR THE
DAY.

Observations

WRITE
DOWN 1 OR 2
OBSERVATIONS
FROM THE
PASSAGE.

Applications

WRITE
DOWN 1 OR 2
APPLICATIONS
FROM THE
PASSAGE.

Pray

WRITE OUT
A PRAYER
OVER WHAT
YOU LEARNED
FROM TODAY'S
PASSAGE.

THURSDAY

Scripture for Week 3

Joshua 8:30-35

30 At that time Joshua built an altar to the Lord, the God of Israel, on Mount Ebal,31 just as Moses the servant of the Lord had commanded the people of Israel, as it is written in the Book of the Law of Moses, "an altar of uncut stones, upon which no man has wielded an iron tool." And they offered on it burnt offerings to the Lordand sacrificed peace offerings. 32 And there, in the presence of the people of Israel, he wrote on the stones a copy of the law of Moses, which he had written.33 And all Israel, sojourner as well as native born, with their elders and officers and their judges, stood on opposite sides of the ark before the Levitical priests who carried the ark of the covenant of the Lord, half of them in front of Mount Gerizim and half of them in front of Mount Ebal, just as Moses the servant of the Lord had commanded at the first, to bless the people of Israel. 34 And afterward he read all the words of the law, the blessing and the curse, according to all that is written in the Book of the Law. 35 There was not a word of all that Moses commanded that Joshua did not read before all the assembly of Israel, and the women, and the little ones, and the sojourners who lived among them.

Deuteronomy 28:1-2

1 "And if you faithfully obey the voice of the Lord your God, being careful to do all his commandments that I command you today, the Lord your God will set you high above all the nations of the earth. 2 And all these blessings shall come upon you and overtake you, if you obey the voice of the Lord your God.

THURSDAY

READ:
Joshua 8:30-35; Deuteronomy 28:1-2

SOAP:
Deuteronomy 28:1-2

Scripture

WRITE
OUT THE
SCRIPTURE
PASSAGE
FOR THE
DAY.

Observations

WRITE
DOWN 1 OR 2
OBSERVATIONS
FROM THE
PASSAGE.

Applications

WRITE
DOWN 1 OR 2
APPLICATIONS
FROM THE
PASSAGE.

Pray

WRITE OUT
A PRAYER
OVER WHAT
YOU LEARNED
FROM TODAY'S
PASSAGE.

FRIDAY

Scripture for Week 3

Joshua 9:1-6; 14-15

1 As soon as all the kings who were beyond the Jordan in the hill country and in the lowland all along the coast of the Great Sea toward Lebanon, the Hittites, the Amorites, the Canaanites, the Perizzites, the Hivites, and the Jebusites, heard of this, 2 they gathered together as one to fight against Joshua and Israel.

3 But when the inhabitants of Gibeon heard what Joshua had done to Jericho and to Ai, 4 they on their part acted with cunning and went and made ready provisions and took worn-out sacks for their donkeys, and wineskins, worn-out and torn and mended, 5 with worn-out, patched sandals on their feet, and worn-out clothes. And all their provisions were dry and crumbly. 6 And they went to Joshua in the camp at Gilgal and said to him and to the men of Israel, "We have come from a distant country, so now make a covenant with us."

14 So the men took some of their provisions, but did not ask counsel from the Lord. 15 And Joshua made peace with them and made a covenant with them, to let them live, and the leaders of the congregation swore to them.

Psalm 33:10-11

10 The Lord brings the counsel of the nations to nothing;
   he frustrates the plans of the peoples.
11 The counsel of the Lord stands forever,
   the plans of his heart to all generations.

FRIDAY

READ:
Joshua 9:1-6; 14-15; Psalm 33:10-11

SOAP:
Psalm 33:10-11

Scripture

WRITE
OUT THE
SCRIPTURE
PASSAGE
FOR THE
DAY.

Observations

WRITE
DOWN 1 OR 2
OBSERVATIONS
FROM THE
PASSAGE.

Applications

WRITE
DOWN 1 OR 2
APPLICATIONS
FROM THE
PASSAGE.

Pray

WRITE OUT
A PRAYER
OVER WHAT
YOU LEARNED
FROM TODAY'S
PASSAGE.

REFLECTION QUESTIONS

1. Achan's steps to sin were "I saw...I coveted...I took." How might the same steps to sin play out today? Is there anything you need to confess the Lord?

2. Are you being obedient to whatever God is asking you to do? If not, why?

3. What's keeping you from being a "Joshua" and living your life in victory?

4. How are obedience and blessing connected?

5. Why is it important to ask for guidance from the Lord before making decisions?

NOTES

WEEK 4

There has been no day like it before or since, when the Lord heeded the voice of a man, for the Lord fought for Israel.

JOSHUA 10:14

PRAYER

Prayer focus for this week:
Spend time praying for your church.

MONDAY

TUESDAY

WEDNESDAY

THURSDAY

FRIDAY

CHALLENGE

You can find this listed in our Monday blog post.

MONDAY
Scripture for Week 4

Joshua 9:22-27

22 Joshua summoned them, and he said to them, "Why did you deceive us, saying, 'We are very far from you,' when you dwell among us? 23 Now therefore you are cursed, and some of you shall never be anything but servants, cutters of wood and drawers of water for the house of my God." 24 They answered Joshua, "Because it was told to your servants for a certainty that the Lord your God had commanded his servant Moses to give you all the land and to destroy all the inhabitants of the land from before you—so we feared greatly for our lives because of you and did this thing. 25 And now, behold, we are in your hand. Whatever seems good and right in your sight to do to us, do it." 26 So he did this to them and delivered them out of the hand of the people of Israel, and they did not kill them. 27 But Joshua made them that day cutters of wood and drawers of water for the congregation and for the altar of the Lord, to this day, in the place that he should choose.

Psalm 19:12-13

12 Who can discern his errors?
　　Declare me innocent from hidden faults.
13 Keep back your servant also from presumptuous sins;
　　let them not have dominion over me!
Then I shall be blameless,
　　and innocent of great transgression.

MONDAY

READ:
Joshua 9:22-27; Psalm 19:12-13

SOAP:
Psalm 19:12-13

Scripture

WRITE
OUT THE
SCRIPTURE
PASSAGE
FOR THE
DAY.

Observations

WRITE
DOWN 1 OR 2
OBSERVATIONS
FROM THE
PASSAGE.

Applications

WRITE
DOWN 1 OR 2
APPLICATIONS
FROM THE
PASSAGE.

Pray

WRITE OUT
A PRAYER
OVER WHAT
YOU LEARNED
FROM TODAY'S
PASSAGE.

TUESDAY
Scripture for Week 4

Joshua 10:12-14; 20-21

12 At that time Joshua spoke to the Lord in the day when
the Lord gave the Amorites over to the sons of Israel, and he said in
the sight of Israel,

"Sun, stand still at Gibeon,
    and moon, in the Valley of Aijalon."

13 And the sun stood still, and the moon stopped,
    until the nation took vengeance on their enemies.

Is this not written in the Book of Jashar? The sun stopped in
the midst of heaven and did not hurry to set for about a whole
day. 14 There has been no day like it before or since, when
the Lord heeded the voice of a man, for the Lord fought for Israel.

20 When Joshua and the sons of Israel had finished striking
them with a great blow until they were wiped out, and when the
remnant that remained of them had entered into the fortified
cities, 21 then all the people returned safe to Joshua in the camp at
Makkedah. Not a man moved his tongue against any of the people
of Israel.

TUESDAY

READ:
Joshua 10:12-14; 20-21

SOAP:
Joshua 10:14

Scripture

WRITE
OUT THE
SCRIPTURE
PASSAGE
FOR THE
DAY.

Observations

WRITE
DOWN 1 OR 2
OBSERVATIONS
FROM THE
PASSAGE.

Applications

WRITE
DOWN 1 OR 2
APPLICATIONS
FROM THE
PASSAGE.

Pray

WRITE OUT
A PRAYER
OVER WHAT
YOU LEARNED
FROM TODAY'S
PASSAGE.

WEDNESDAY
Scripture for Week 4

Joshua 10:38-43

38 Then Joshua and all Israel with him turned back to Debir and fought against it39 and he captured it with its king and all its towns. And they struck them with the edge of the sword and devoted to destruction every person in it; he left none remaining. Just as he had done to Hebron and to Libnah and its king, so he did to Debir and to its king.

40 So Joshua struck the whole land, the hill country and the Negeb and the lowland and the slopes, and all their kings. He left none remaining, but devoted to destruction all that breathed, just as the Lord God of Israel commanded. 41 And Joshua struck them from Kadesh-barnea as far as Gaza, and all the country of Goshen, as far as Gibeon. 42 And Joshua captured all these kings and their land at one time, because the Lord God of Israel fought for Israel. 43 Then Joshua returned, and all Israel with him, to the camp at Gilgal.

Jeremiah 1:19

19 They will fight against you, but they shall not prevail against you, for I am with you, declares the Lord, to deliver you."

WEDNESDAY

READ:
Joshua 10:38-43; Jeremiah 1:19

SOAP:
Jeremiah 1:19

Scripture

WRITE
OUT THE
SCRIPTURE
PASSAGE
FOR THE
DAY.

Observations

WRITE
DOWN 1 OR 2
OBSERVATIONS
FROM THE
PASSAGE.

Applications

WRITE
DOWN 1 OR 2
APPLICATIONS
FROM THE
PASSAGE.

Pray

WRITE OUT
A PRAYER
OVER WHAT
YOU LEARNED
FROM TODAY'S
PASSAGE.

THURSDAY

Scripture for Week 4

Joshua 11:3-10

3 to the Canaanites in the east and the west, the Amorites, the Hittites, the Perizzites, and the Jebusites in the hill country, and the Hivites under Hermon in the land of Mizpah. 4 And they came out with all their troops, a great horde, in number like the sand that is on the seashore, with very many horses and chariots.5 And all these kings joined their forces and came and encamped together at the waters of Merom to fight against Israel.

6 And the Lord said to Joshua, "Do not be afraid of them, for tomorrow at this time I will give over all of them, slain, to Israel. You shall hamstring their horses and burn their chariots with fire." 7 So Joshua and all his warriors came suddenly against them by the waters of Merom and fell upon them. 8 And the Lord gave them into the hand of Israel, who struck them and chased them as far as Great Sidon and Misrephoth-maim, and eastward as far as the Valley of Mizpeh. And they struck them until he left none remaining. 9 And Joshua did to them just as the Lord said to him: he hamstrung their horses and burned their chariots with fire.

10 And Joshua turned back at that time and captured Hazor and struck its king with the sword, for Hazor formerly was the head of all those kingdoms.

2 Kings 6:16-17

16 He said, "Do not be afraid, for those who are with us are more than those who are with them." 17 Then Elisha prayed and said, "O Lord, please open his eyes that he may see." So the Lord opened the eyes of the young man, and he saw, and behold, the mountain was full of horses and chariots of fire all around Elisha.

THURSDAY

READ:
Joshua 11:3-10; 2 Kings 6:16-17

SOAP:
2 Kings 6:16

Scripture

WRITE
OUT THE
SCRIPTURE
PASSAGE
FOR THE
DAY.

Observations

WRITE
DOWN 1 OR 2
OBSERVATIONS
FROM THE
PASSAGE.

Applications

WRITE
DOWN 1 OR 2
APPLICATIONS
FROM THE
PASSAGE.

Pray

WRITE OUT
A PRAYER
OVER WHAT
YOU LEARNED
FROM TODAY'S
PASSAGE.

FRIDAY
Scripture for Week 4

Joshua 13:1-8

Now Joshua was old and advanced in years, and the Lord said to him, "You are old and advanced in years, and there remains yet very much land to possess.2 This is the land that yet remains: all the regions of the Philistines, and all those of the Geshurites 3 (from the Shihor, which is east of Egypt, northward to the boundary of Ekron, it is counted as Canaanite; there are five rulers of the Philistines, those of Gaza, Ashdod, Ashkelon, Gath, and Ekron), and those of the Avvim, 4 in the south, all the land of the Canaanites, and Mearah that belongs to the Sidonians, to Aphek, to the boundary of the Amorites, 5 and the land of the Gebalites, and all Lebanon, toward the sunrise, from Baal-gad below Mount Hermon to Lebo-hamath, 6 all the inhabitants of the hill country from Lebanon to Misrephoth-maim, even all the Sidonians. I myself will drive them out from before the people of Israel. Only allot the land to Israel for an inheritance, as I have commanded you. 7 Now therefore divide this land for an inheritance to the nine tribes and half the tribe of Manasseh."

8 With the other half of the tribe of Manasseh the Reubenites and the Gadites received their inheritance, which Moses gave them, beyond the Jordan eastward, as Moses the servant of the Lord gave them.

Isaiah 66:3-4

3 "He who slaughters an ox is like one who kills a man;
    he who sacrifices a lamb, like one who breaks a dog's neck;
he who presents a grain offering, like one who offers pig's blood;
    he who makes a memorial offering of frankincense, like one who blesses an idol.
These have chosen their own ways,
    and their soul delights in their abominations;
4 I also will choose harsh treatment for them
    and bring their fears upon them,
because when I called, no one answered,
    when I spoke, they did not listen;
but they did what was evil in my eyes
    and chose that in which I did not delight."

FRIDAY

READ:
Joshua 13:1-8; Isaiah 66:3-4

SOAP:
Isaiah 66:3-4

Scripture

WRITE
OUT THE
SCRIPTURE
PASSAGE
FOR THE
DAY.

Observations

WRITE
DOWN 1 OR 2
OBSERVATIONS
FROM THE
PASSAGE.

Applications

WRITE
DOWN 1 OR 2
APPLICATIONS
FROM THE
PASSAGE.

Pray

WRITE OUT
A PRAYER
OVER WHAT
YOU LEARNED
FROM TODAY'S
PASSAGE.

REFLECTION QUESTIONS

1. How can we avoid making the same mistake Joshua did with the Gibeonites?

2. What contributed to Joshua's success in the battle (Joshua 10)?

3. Do you have times when you feel that God is not with you? How do today's verses show you that God is always by your side?

4. How can we open our spiritual eyes to the things God is doing in our lives?

5. How can we make good choices? How can we avoid making bad choices?

NOTES

WEEK 5

So now give me this hill country
of which the Lord spoke on that day,
for you heard on that day how
the Anakim were there, with great
fortified cities. It may be that
the Lord will be with me, and I shall
drive them out just as the Lord said.

JOSHUA 14:12

PRAYER

Prayer focus for this week:
Spend time praying for missionaries.

MONDAY

TUESDAY

WEDNESDAY

THURSDAY

FRIDAY

CHALLENGE
You can find this listed in our Monday blog post.

MONDAY
Scripture for Week 5

Joshua 14:6-13

6 Then the people of Judah came to Joshua at Gilgal. And Caleb the son of Jephunneh the Kenizzite said to him, "You know what the Lord said to Moses the man of God in Kadesh-barnea concerning you and me. 7 I was forty years old when Moses the servant of the Lord sent me from Kadesh-barnea to spy out the land, and I brought him word again as it was in my heart. 8 But my brothers who went up with me made the heart of the people melt; yet I wholly followed the Lord my God. 9 And Moses swore on that day, saying, 'Surely the land on which your foot has trodden shall be an inheritance for you and your children forever, because you have wholly followed the Lord my God.' 10 And now, behold, the Lord has kept me alive, just as he said, these forty-five years since the time that the Lord spoke this word to Moses, while Israel walked in the wilderness. And now, behold, I am this day eighty-five years old. 11 I am still as strong today as I was in the day that Moses sent me; my strength now is as my strength was then, for war and for going and coming. 12 So now give me this hill country of which the Lord spoke on that day, for you heard on that day how the Anakim were there, with great fortified cities. It may be that the Lord will be with me, and I shall drive them out just as the Lord said."

13 Then Joshua blessed him, and he gave Hebron to Caleb the son of Jephunneh for an inheritance.

MONDAY

READ:
Joshua 14:6-13

SOAP:
Joshua 14:12

Scripture

WRITE
OUT THE
SCRIPTURE
PASSAGE
FOR THE
DAY.

Observations

WRITE
DOWN 1 OR 2
OBSERVATIONS
FROM THE
PASSAGE.

Applications

WRITE
DOWN 1 OR 2
APPLICATIONS
FROM THE
PASSAGE.

Pray

WRITE OUT
A PRAYER
OVER WHAT
YOU LEARNED
FROM TODAY'S
PASSAGE.

TUESDAY
Scripture for Week 5

Joshua 17:12-18

12 Yet the people of Manasseh could not take possession of those cities, but the Canaanites persisted in dwelling in that land. 13 Now when the people of Israel grew strong, they put the Canaanites to forced labor, but did not utterly drive them out.

14 Then the people of Joseph spoke to Joshua, saying, "Why have you given me but one lot and one portion as an inheritance, although I am a numerous people, since all along the Lord has blessed me?" 15 And Joshua said to them, "If you are a numerous people, go up by yourselves to the forest, and there clear ground for yourselves in the land of the Perizzites and the Rephaim, since the hill country of Ephraim is too narrow for you." 16 The people of Joseph said, "The hill country is not enough for us. Yet all the Canaanites who dwell in the plain have chariots of iron, both those in Beth-shean and its villages and those in the Valley of Jezreel."17 Then Joshua said to the house of Joseph, to Ephraim and Manasseh, "You are a numerous people and have great power. You shall not have one allotment only,18 but the hill country shall be yours, for though it is a forest, you shall clear it and possess it to its farthest borders. For you shall drive out the Canaanites, though they have chariots of iron, and though they are strong."

1 Corinthians 5:6-8

6 Your boasting is not good. Do you not know that a little leaven leavens the whole lump? 7 Cleanse out the old leaven that you may be a new lump, as you really are unleavened. For Christ, our Passover lamb, has been sacrificed. 8 Let us therefore celebrate the festival, not with the old leaven, the leaven of malice and evil, but with the unleavened bread of sincerity and truth.

James 4:16

16 As it is, you boast in your arrogance. All such boasting is evil.

TUESDAY

READ:
Joshua 17:12-18; 1 Corinthians 5:6-8; James 4:16

SOAP:
1 Corinthians 5:6-8

Scripture

WRITE
OUT THE
SCRIPTURE
PASSAGE
FOR THE
DAY.

Observations

WRITE
DOWN 1 OR 2
OBSERVATIONS
FROM THE
PASSAGE.

Applications

WRITE
DOWN 1 OR 2
APPLICATIONS
FROM THE
PASSAGE.

Pray

WRITE OUT
A PRAYER
OVER WHAT
YOU LEARNED
FROM TODAY'S
PASSAGE.

WEDNESDAY
Scripture for Week 5

Joshua 18:1-10

1 Then the whole congregation of the people of Israel assembled at Shiloh and set up the tent of meeting there. The land lay subdued before them.

2 There remained among the people of Israel seven tribes whose inheritance had not yet been apportioned. 3 So Joshua said to the people of Israel, "How long will you put off going in to take possession of the land, which the Lord, the God of your fathers, has given you? 4 Provide three men from each tribe, and I will send them out that they may set out and go up and down the land. They shall write a description of it with a view to their inheritances, and then come to me. 5 They shall divide it into seven portions. Judah shall continue in his territory on the south, and the house of Joseph shall continue in their territory on the north. 6 And you shall describe the land in seven divisions and bring the description here to me. And I will cast lots for you here before the Lord our God. 7 The Levites have no portion among you, for the priesthood of the Lord is their heritage. And Gad and Reuben and half the tribe of Manasseh have received their inheritance beyond the Jordan eastward, which Moses the servant of the Lord gave them."

8 So the men arose and went, and Joshua charged those who went to write the description of the land, saying, "Go up and down in the land and write a description and return to me. And I will cast lots for you here before the Lord in Shiloh." 9 So the men went and passed up and down in the land and wrote in a book a description of it by towns in seven divisions. Then they came to Joshua to the camp at Shiloh, 10 and Joshua cast lots for them in Shiloh before the Lord. And there Joshua apportioned the land to the people of Israel, to each his portion.

Proverbs 10:4

4 A slack hand causes poverty,
   but the hand of the diligent makes rich.

WEDNESDAY

READ:
Joshua 18:1-10; Proverbs 10:4

SOAP:
Proverbs 10:4

Scripture

WRITE
OUT THE
SCRIPTURE
PASSAGE
FOR THE
DAY.

Observations

WRITE
DOWN 1 OR 2
OBSERVATIONS
FROM THE
PASSAGE.

Applications

WRITE
DOWN 1 OR 2
APPLICATIONS
FROM THE
PASSAGE.

Pray

WRITE OUT
A PRAYER
OVER WHAT
YOU LEARNED
FROM TODAY'S
PASSAGE.

THURSDAY
Scripture for Week 5

Joshua 20:1-6
1 Then the Lord said to Joshua, 2 "Say to the people of
Israel, 'Appoint the cities of refuge, of which I spoke to you through
Moses, 3 that the manslayer who strikes any person without intent
or unknowingly may flee there. They shall be for you a refuge from
the avenger of blood. 4 He shall flee to one of these cities and shall
stand at the entrance of the gate of the city and explain his case
to the elders of that city. Then they shall take him into the city
and give him a place, and he shall remain with them. 5 And if the
avenger of blood pursues him, they shall not give up the manslayer
into his hand, because he struck his neighbor unknowingly, and did
not hate him in the past. 6 And he shall remain in that city until he
has stood before the congregation for judgment, until the death of
him who is high priest at the time. Then the manslayer may return
to his own town and his own home, to the town from which he
fled.'"

Hebrews 6:18
18 so that by two unchangeable things, in which it is impossible
for God to lie, we who have fled for refuge might have strong
encouragement to hold fast to the hope set before us.

Psalm 94:21-22
21 They band together against the life of the righteous
   and condemn the innocent to death.
22 But the Lord has become my stronghold,
   and my God the rock of my refuge.

THURSDAY

READ:
Joshua 20:1-6; Hebrews 6:18; Psalm 94:21-22

SOAP:
Psalm 94:22

Scripture

WRITE
OUT THE
SCRIPTURE
PASSAGE
FOR THE
DAY.

Observations

WRITE
DOWN 1 OR 2
OBSERVATIONS
FROM THE
PASSAGE.

Applications

WRITE
DOWN 1 OR 2
APPLICATIONS
FROM THE
PASSAGE.

Pray

WRITE OUT
A PRAYER
OVER WHAT
YOU LEARNED
FROM TODAY'S
PASSAGE.

FRIDAY

Scripture for Week 5

Joshua 21:1-3

1 Then the heads of the fathers' houses of the Levites came to
Eleazar the priest and to Joshua the son of Nun and to the
heads of the fathers' houses of the tribes of the people of
Israel. 2 And they said to them at Shiloh in the land of
Canaan, "The Lord commanded through Moses that we be
given cities to dwell in, along with their pasturelands for our
livestock." 3 So by command of the Lord the people of Israel gave
to the Levites the following cities and pasturelands out of their
inheritance.

2 Chronicles 17:7-9

7 In the third year of his reign he sent his officials, Ben-hail,
Obadiah, Zechariah, Nethanel, and Micaiah, to teach in the cities
of Judah; 8 and with them the Levites, Shemaiah, Nethaniah,
Zebadiah, Asahel, Shemiramoth, Jehonathan, Adonijah, Tobijah,
and Tobadonijah; and with these Levites, the priests Elishama and
Jehoram. 9 And they taught in Judah, having the Book of the Law
of the Lord with them. They went about through all the cities of
Judah and taught among the people.

Nehemiah 8:7-8

7 Also Jeshua, Bani, Sherebiah, Jamin, Akkub, Shabbethai,
Hodiah, Maaseiah, Kelita, Azariah, Jozabad, Hanan, Pelaiah, the
Levites, helped the people to understand the Law, while the people
remained in their places. 8 They read from the book, from the
Law of God, clearly, and they gave the sense, so that the people
understood the reading.

Psalm 119:27

27 Make me understand the way of your precepts,
   and I will meditate on your wondrous works.

FRIDAY

READ:
Joshua 21:1-3; 2 Chronicles 17:7-9; Nehemiah 8:7-8; Psalm 119:27

SOAP:
Psalm 119:27

Scripture

WRITE
OUT THE
SCRIPTURE
PASSAGE
FOR THE
DAY.

Observations

WRITE
DOWN 1 OR 2
OBSERVATIONS
FROM THE
PASSAGE.

Applications

WRITE
DOWN 1 OR 2
APPLICATIONS
FROM THE
PASSAGE.

Pray

WRITE OUT
A PRAYER
OVER WHAT
YOU LEARNED
FROM TODAY'S
PASSAGE.

REFLECTION QUESTIONS

1. Are you asking the Lord to show you how you can serve Him? What work has He prepared for you?

2. The sons of Joseph complained because the Lord didn't give them enough room. How does pride get in your way to accept God's will for your life?

3. Seven tribes put off taking possession of the land until Joshua called them to do it. What areas of your spiritual life are you neglecting? How can you change that?

4. What are some comparisons and contrasts between cities of refuge and our salvation in Jesus Christ?

5. The Levites were a godly influence for the rest of tribes of Israel. How can you be of godly influence to those around you?

NOTES

WEEK 6

And if it is evil in your eyes to serve the Lord, choose this day whom you will serve, whether the gods your fathers served in the region beyond the River, or the gods of the Amorites in whose land you dwell. But as for me and my house, we will serve the Lord.

JOSHUA 24:15

PRAYER

Prayer focus for this week:
Spend time praying for yourself.

MONDAY

TUESDAY

WEDNESDAY

THURSDAY

FRIDAY

CHALLENGE

You can find this listed in our Monday blog post.

MONDAY
Scripture for Week 6

Joshua 21:43-45

43 Thus the Lord gave to Israel all the land that he swore to give to their fathers. And they took possession of it, and they settled there. 44 And the Lord gave them rest on every side just as he had sworn to their fathers. Not one of all their enemies had withstood them, for the Lord had given all their enemies into their hands. 45 Not one word of all the good promises that the Lord had made to the house of Israel had failed; all came to pass.

MONDAY

READ:
Joshua 21:43-45

SOAP:
Joshua 21:45

Scripture

WRITE
OUT THE
SCRIPTURE
PASSAGE
FOR THE
DAY.

Observations

WRITE
DOWN 1 OR 2
OBSERVATIONS
FROM THE
PASSAGE.

Applications

WRITE
DOWN 1 OR 2
APPLICATIONS
FROM THE
PASSAGE.

Pray

WRITE OUT
A PRAYER
OVER WHAT
YOU LEARNED
FROM TODAY'S
PASSAGE.

TUESDAY
Scripture for Week 6

Joshua 22:1-6
1 At that time Joshua summoned the Reubenites and the Gadites and the half-tribe of Manasseh, 2 and said to them, "You have kept all that Moses the servant of the Lord commanded you and have obeyed my voice in all that I have commanded you. 3 You have not forsaken your brothers these many days, down to this day, but have been careful to keep the charge of the Lord your God. 4 And now the Lord your God has given rest to your brothers, as he promised them. Therefore turn and go to your tents in the land where your possession lies, which Moses the servant of the Lord gave you on the other side of the Jordan. 5 Only be very careful to observe the commandment and the law that Moses the servant of the Lord commanded you, to love the Lord your God, and to walk in all his ways and to keep his commandments and to cling to him and to serve him with all your heart and with all your soul." 6 So Joshua blessed them and sent them away, and they went to their tents.

Matthew 22:36-38
36 "Teacher, which is the great commandment in the Law?" 37 And he said to him, "You shall love the Lord your God with all your heart and with all your soul and with all your mind. 38 This is the great and first commandment.

John 14:15
15 "If you love me, you will keep my commandments.

TUESDAY

READ:
Joshua 22:1-6; Matthew 22:36-38; John 14:15

SOAP:
John 14:15

Scripture

WRITE
OUT THE
SCRIPTURE
PASSAGE
FOR THE
DAY.

Observations

WRITE
DOWN 1 OR 2
OBSERVATIONS
FROM THE
PASSAGE.

Applications

WRITE
DOWN 1 OR 2
APPLICATIONS
FROM THE
PASSAGE.

Pray

WRITE OUT
A PRAYER
OVER WHAT
YOU LEARNED
FROM TODAY'S
PASSAGE.

WEDNESDAY
Scripture for Week 6

Joshua 23:6-12

6 Therefore, be very strong to keep and to do all that is written in the Book of the Law of Moses, turning aside from it neither to the right hand nor to the left, 7 that you may not mix with these nations remaining among you or make mention of the names of their gods or swear by them or serve them or bow down to them, 8 but you shall cling to the Lord your God just as you have done to this day. 9 For the Lord has driven out before you great and strong nations. And as for you, no man has been able to stand before you to this day. 10 One man of you puts to flight a thousand, since it is the Lord your God who fights for you, just as he promised you. 11 Be very careful, therefore, to love the Lord your God. 12 For if you turn back and cling to the remnant of these nations remaining among you and make marriages with them, so that you associate with them and they with you,

WEDNESDAY

READ:
Joshua 23:6-12

SOAP:
Joshua 23:8

Scripture

WRITE
OUT THE
SCRIPTURE
PASSAGE
FOR THE
DAY.

Observations

WRITE
DOWN 1 OR 2
OBSERVATIONS
FROM THE
PASSAGE.

Applications

WRITE
DOWN 1 OR 2
APPLICATIONS
FROM THE
PASSAGE.

Pray

WRITE OUT
A PRAYER
OVER WHAT
YOU LEARNED
FROM TODAY'S
PASSAGE.

THURSDAY
Scripture for Week 6

Joshua 24:11-15

11 And you went over the Jordan and came to Jericho, and the leaders of Jericho fought against you, and also the Amorites, the Perizzites, the Canaanites, the Hittites, the Girgashites, the Hivites, and the Jebusites. And I gave them into your hand. 12 And I sent the hornet before you, which drove them out before you, the two kings of the Amorites; it was not by your sword or by your bow. 13 I gave you a land on which you had not labored and cities that you had not built, and you dwell in them. You eat the fruit of vineyards and olive orchards that you did not plant.'

14 "Now therefore fear the Lord and serve him in sincerity and in faithfulness. Put away the gods that your fathers served beyond the River and in Egypt, and serve the Lord. 15 And if it is evil in your eyes to serve the Lord, choose this day whom you will serve, whether the gods your fathers served in the region beyond the River, or the gods of the Amorites in whose land you dwell. But as for me and my house, we will serve the Lord."

THURSDAY

READ:
Joshua 24:11-15

SOAP:
Joshua 24:15

Scripture

WRITE
OUT THE
SCRIPTURE
PASSAGE
FOR THE
DAY.

Observations

WRITE
DOWN 1 OR 2
OBSERVATIONS
FROM THE
PASSAGE.

Applications

WRITE
DOWN 1 OR 2
APPLICATIONS
FROM THE
PASSAGE.

Pray

WRITE OUT
A PRAYER
OVER WHAT
YOU LEARNED
FROM TODAY'S
PASSAGE.

FRIDAY
Scripture for Week 6

Joshua 24:19-23
19 But Joshua said to the people, "You are not able to serve
the Lord, for he is a holy God. He is a jealous God; he will
not forgive your transgressions or your sins. 20 If you forsake
the Lord and serve foreign gods, then he will turn and do you
harm and consume you, after having done you good." 21 And the
people said to Joshua, "No, but we will serve the Lord." 22 Then
Joshua said to the people, "You are witnesses against yourselves
that you have chosen the Lord, to serve him." And they said, "We
are witnesses." 23 He said, "Then put away the foreign gods that are
among you, and incline your heart to the Lord, the God of Israel."

2 Timothy 2:20-21
20 Now in a great house there are not only vessels of gold and
silver but also of wood and clay, some for honorable use, some for
dishonorable. 21 Therefore, if anyone cleanses himself from what is
dishonorable, he will be a vessel for honorable use, set apart as holy,
useful to the master of the house, ready for every good work.

FRIDAY

READ:
Joshua 24:19-23; 2 Timothy 2:20-21

SOAP:
2 Timothy 2:21

Scripture

WRITE
OUT THE
SCRIPTURE
PASSAGE
FOR THE
DAY.

Observations

WRITE
DOWN 1 OR 2
OBSERVATIONS
FROM THE
PASSAGE.

Applications

WRITE
DOWN 1 OR 2
APPLICATIONS
FROM THE
PASSAGE.

Pray

WRITE OUT
A PRAYER
OVER WHAT
YOU LEARNED
FROM TODAY'S
PASSAGE.

REFLECTION
QUESTIONS

1. What promises has God fulfilled in your life? Spend time praying in gratitude and praise today.

2. What does your obedience to God say about your love for Him? Are you taking responsibility for your spiritual growth?

3. Why do you think today's verses say that we have to be very strong to keep and do God's Word?

4. How are you and your house serving God? What can you do to improve your service?

5. Analyze today what kind of "vessel" you are. How can you apply the spiritual principles you've learned in the book of Joshua?

NOTES

KNOW THESE TRUTHS
from God's Word

God loves you.
Even when you're feeling unworthy and like the world is stacked against you, God loves you - yes, you - and He has created you for great purpose.

God's Word says, "God so loved the world that He gave His one and only Son, Jesus, that whoever believes in Him shall not perish, but have eternal life" (John 3:16).

Our sin separates us from God.
We are all sinners by nature and by choice, and because of this we are separated from God, who is holy.

God's Word says, "All have sinned and fall short of the glory of God" (Romans 3:23).

Jesus died so that you might have life.
The consequence of sin is death, but your story doesn't have to end there! God's free gift of salvation is available to us because Jesus took the penalty for our sin when He died on the cross.

God's Word says, "For the wages of sin is death, but the free gift of God is eternal life in Christ Jesus our Lord" (Romans 6:23); "God demonstrates His own love toward us, in that while we were yet sinners, Christ died for us" (Romans 5:8).

Jesus lives!
Death could not hold Him, and three days after His body was placed in the tomb Jesus rose again, defeating sin and death forever! He lives today in heaven and is preparing a place in eternity for all who believe in Him.

God's Word says, "In my Father's house are many rooms. If it were not so, would I have told you that I go to prepare a place for you? And if I go and prepare a place for you, I will come again and will take you to myself, that where I am you may be also" (John 14:2-3).

Yes, you can KNOW that you are forgiven.
Accept Jesus as the only way to salvation...

Accepting Jesus as your Savior is not about what you can do, but rather about having faith in what Jesus has already done. It takes recognizing that you are a sinner, believing that Jesus died for your sins, and asking for forgiveness by placing your full trust in Jesus's work on the cross on your behalf.

God's Word says, "If you confess with your mouth that Jesus is Lord and believe in your heart that God raised him from the dead, you will be saved. For with the heart one believes and is justified, and with the mouth one confesses and is saved" (Romans 10:9-10).

Practically, what does that look like?
With a sincere heart, you can pray a simple prayer like this:

God,
I know that I am a sinner.
I don't want to live another day without embracing
the love and forgiveness that You have for me.
I ask for Your forgiveness.
I believe that You died for my sins and rose from the dead.
I surrender all that I am and ask You to be Lord of my life.
Help me to turn from my sin and follow You.
Teach me what it means to walk in freedom as I live under Your grace,
and help me to grow in Your ways as I seek to know You more.
Amen.

If you just prayed this prayer (or something similar in your own words), would you email us at info@lovegodgreatly.com?

We'd love to help get you started on this exciting journey as a child of God!

WELCOME FRIEND

We're so glad you're here

Love God Greatly exists to inspire, encourage, and equip women all over the world to make God's Word a priority in their lives.

INSPIRE

women to make God's Word a priority in their daily lives through our Bible study resources.

ENCOURAGE

women in their daily walks with God through online community and personal accountability.

EQUIP

women to grow in their faith, so that they can effectively reach others for Christ.

Love God Greatly consists of a beautiful community of women who use a variety of technology platforms to keep each other accountable in God's Word.

We start with a simple Bible reading plan, but it doesn't stop there.

Some gather in homes and churches locally, while others connect online with women across the globe. Whatever the method, we lovingly lock arms and unite for this purpose...to Love God Greatly with our lives.

At Love God Greatly, you'll find real, authentic women. Women who are imperfect, yet forgiven. Women who desire less of us, and a whole lot more of Jesus. Women who long to know God through his Word, because we know that Truth transforms and sets us free. Women who are better together, saturated in God's Word and in community with one another.

Love God Greatly is a 501 (C) (3) non-profit organization. Funding for Love God Greatly comes through donations and proceeds from our online Bible study journals and books. LGG is committed to providing quality Bible study materials and believes finances should never get in the way of a woman being able to participate in one of our studies. All journals and translated journals are available to download for free from LoveGodGreatly.com for those who cannot afford to purchase them. Our journals and books are also available for sale on Amazon. Search for "Love God Greatly" to see all of our Bible study journals and books. 100% of proceeds go directly back into supporting Love God Greatly and helping us inspire, encourage and equip women all over the world with God's Word.

THANK YOU for partnering with us!

WHAT WE OFFER:

18 + Translations | Bible Reading Plans | Online Bible Study
Love God Greatly App | 80 + Countries Served
Bible Study Journals & Books | Community Groups

EACH LGG STUDY INCLUDES:

Three Devotional Corresponding Blog Posts
Memory Verses | Weekly Challenge | Weekly Reading Plan
Reflection Questions And More!

OTHER LOVE GOD GREATLY STUDIES INCLUDE:

Savior | Promises of God | Love the Loveless | Truth Over Lies
1 & 2 Thessalonians | Fear & Anxiety | James | His Name Is...
Philippians | 1 & 2 Timothy | Sold Out | Ruth | Broken & Redeemed
Walking in Wisdom | God With Us | In Everything Give Thanks
You Are Forgiven | David | Ecclesiastes | Growing Through Prayer
Names of God | Galatians | Psalm 119 | 1st & 2nd Peter
Made For Community | The Road To Christmas
The Source Of Gratitude | Esther | You Are Loved

Visit us online at
LOVEGODGREATLY.COM

Made in the USA
Columbia, SC
04 June 2019